Diet recommendations for Diverticulitis

Please check these recommendations always with a nutrition consultant, therapist, doctor or dietician. The recipes and the list of ingredients are supporting the conventional medical therapy.
The calorie disclosures of fresh ingredients (fruit and vegetables) vary according to quality and time of harvest. The contents were checked by a dietician and a nutrition consultant for the Traditional Chinese Medicine (TCM).

Author:
©2017 Josef Miligui
www.ebns.at

AF190373

Source:
The lists are created from the EBNS database for nutritional counseling. The database is used by dietitians, therapists and doctors for advising the patient / client.

Literature:
The specialist literature and the training documents of the German and Austrian dietary and traditional Chinese medicine serve as a knowledge base. We have used the documents as a basis of knowledge, adapted it to our experience and completed them.
http://di-book.com

Title Photo:
©2008 Erika Weixlbaumer

Production and publishing:
BoD – Books on Demand, Norderstedt
ISBN: 9783746036663

Diet recommendations for DIETETICS - Gastrointestinal tract - Small intestine and large intestine - Diverticulitis

1   Treatment strategy

The therapy of diverticulitis begins with a fasting period. To alleviate the complaints, fibre-rich diet has proved successful.
Especially fibre from cereals is recommended. It is for example contained in whole-grain bread, bran and blending's of muesli. As to most of the premade blending's of muesli sugar is added, it is recommended to prepare the muesli oneself.
Also nuts and almonds fit well in the diet.
----- Especially healthy for you are potatoes, fruits, salad and vegetables, especially legumes (peas, beans), as they contain a lot of fibre. If you have been eating little whole-grain products so far, your intestines must get used to the change of nutrition.

During the transition period - it takes about a week - a slight abdominal pain and bloating may occur.

Furthermore you should drink as much as possible, at least 2 litres a day! This additionally supports your digestion.

------- Milk- and fruit acid (contained in yogurt or apples) promote intestinal activity.
Also physical exercise is recommended to stimulate the digestion.
A problem concerning the diet could be indigestible grains and pips as linseed, raspberry seeds etc., because they can be hardly chewed and then they can become entangled in the diverticula and so can trigger infections.

2   Avoid

Avoid white flour products, sugar and a bigger amount of meat, sausage, cheese and fish. These foods are not appropriate for you, because they contain only little fibre.
Avoid grains.
Do you easily tend to constipation? Then additionally you should avoid all kinds of food, which have a constipating effect. These are for example string black tea, red wine, cacao as well as cacao containing foods.

3 Breakfast

4 Snack

5 Lunch

6 Afternoon

7 Dinner

8 Any time

9 Recipes

(recommended) = You can use more.
(little) = You should use less than specified or omit.

9.1 Banana Soymilk

Good to fight loss of appetite, oral mucosa inflammation. Strengthens body energy, promotes stomach-spleen harmony, promotes digestion, regulates gastrointestinal function. Relieves pain, detoxifying, bactericide.

Cooking time approx. 5 min
Calories p. portion: 126
2 portions
Allergens: E

Quantity of ingredients
Banana 1 piece / 120g. (recommended)
Cinnamon ground 1 pinch / 1g. (yes)
Soybean milk 1 1/2 cups / 400g. (little)
Honey 1 teaspoon / 3g. (little)
Acerola fruit nectar or powder 1 teaspoon / 2g. (little)

Cooking instructions:
Cut the banana into pieces, puree them with soy milk, acerola, honey and cinnamon with the mixing stick.

9.2 Barley soup

Diuretic, forcing spleen, supports urination, stimulates liver function, antioxidativ, promotes digestion, detoxifying, reduces blood lipids, stimulates, dissolves stagnation.

Cooking time approx. 25 min
Calories p. portion: 265
2 portions
Allergens: A

Quantity of ingredients
Water 1 1/2 cups / 240g. (yes)
Olive oil 1 table spoon / 10g. (little)
Parsley 2 table spoons / 30g. (recommended)

Barley 1 cup / 120g. (yes)
Salt 1 pinch / 1g. (little)
Ginger fresh 1/2 teaspoon / 1g. (little)

Cooking instructions:
Roast the barley in the pan, then grind it to the ground, and boil with water, some salt and ginger to a mash. Before serving add oil and parsley.

Variant: You can add a better taste to the dish if you cook it with prepared vegetable or meat broth.

9.3   Basic recipe for a chicken broth worming

Strengthens blood, strengthens bone marrow, reduces blood pressure, strengthens immune system, prevents cancer, reduces radiation damage, promotes sweating, dissolves stagnation, good to fight loss of appetite.

Cooking time approx. 2-3 hours
Calories p. portion: 90
9 portions
Allergens: L

Quantity of ingredients
Celery root 1 piece / 500g. (recommended)
Juniper berry 1 teaspoon / 3g. (yes)
Bay leaf 3 pieces / 2g. (yes)
Chicken meat 1/2 piece / 600g. (little)
Fenugreek (Trigonella foenum-graecum) 1 teaspoon / 2g. (yes)
Carrot 2 pieces / 150g. (recommended)
Leek 1 stick / 45g. ()
Ginger fresh 2 slices / 2g. (little)
Water 4 cup / 900g. (yes)

Cooking instructions:
Remove chicken parts from fat. Place chicken pieces in a saucepan with hot water and heat till it boils briefly, skimming any resulting foam. Add coarsely chopped vegetables and all spices and cook over medium heat for 2 to 3 hours. Strain the finished soup. Throw away vegetables and bones.

Tip: If you want to use the meat as a soup insert, take out after 45 minutes and return only the bones in the soup.
Refrigerate for later use.

9.4 Basic recipe for a reissue soup (Congee)

Low fat content, for the drainage of the body overweight and high blood pressure.

Cooking time approx. 2-4 hours
Calories p. portion: 140
3 portions
Allergens: -

Quantity of ingredients
Rice variety any 1 cup / 120g. (yes)
Water 6 cups / 700g. (yes)

Cooking instructions:
Cook rice and water in a ratio of about 1: 6. The amount of water determines the thickness of the mash (matter of taste).
Put the rice in a saucepan with a heavy lid. It is important to simmer the rice after a short boil on the slightest flame, otherwise it burns.
Boil the rice for 2-4 hours. The longer he cooks, the more he strengthens.
If you want to eat the dish for breakfast, you can put the rice on just before bedtime.
To be on the safe side, you should first check the behavior of your pot and cooker under observation for a similar amount of time, so that nothing burns.
Refrigerate for later use.

9.5 Basic recipe for a vegetable soup, nutritious

Reduces blood pressure, strengthens immune system, prevents cancer, forcing spleen, dissolves stagnation, promotes weight loss. Good to fight immunodeficiency, high blood pressure, depressions, diabetes, diarrhea, reduces blood lipids.

Cooking time approx. 2-3 hours

Calories p. portion: 48
5 portions
Allergens: L

Quantity of ingredients
Lovage 1 table spoon / 3g. (recommended)
Salt 1 pinch / 1g. (little)
Thyme dried 1 pinch / 1g. (yes)
Olive oil 1 table spoon / 4g. (little)
Ginger fresh 1/2 teaspoon / 2g. (little)
Juniper berry 6 pieces / 6g. (yes)
Parsnip 3/8 lbs - 6oz / 150g. (yes)
Lemon 1/2 piece / 25g. ()
Celery root 1 cup / 100g. (recommended)
Water 3 cups / 650g. (yes)
Carrot 3 pieces / 200g. (recommended)
Bay leaf 2 leaves / 1g. (yes)
Onion white 1 piece / 60g. ()

Cooking instructions:
Cut the vegetables into cubes.
Heat oil in hot pot, fry shortly onions and vegetables.
Add cold water, then add ginger, bay leaf and lemon juice.
Season with juniper, thyme and lovage. Cover for 2 - 3 hours on a low heat and simmer.
The used vegetables should be thrown away.
The basic recipe serves as a soup base and to refine vegetables, legumes or cereals.
If you want to eat vegetable soup immediately, add the desired vegetables half an hour before.
Refrigerate for later use.

9.6   Basmati rice + Zucchini tofu dish

Diuretic, supports urination, harmonizes spleen and stomach, reduces flatulence, good to fight body overweight and high blood pressure. Antioxidativ, promotes digestion, perspiration, reduces blood lipids, forcing spleen.

Cooking time approx. 20 min
Calories p. portion: 146

4 portions
Allergens: E

Quantity of ingredients
Zucchini 1 piece / 700g. (recommended)
Rice Basmati 1/2 cup / 60g. (yes)
Coriander 1/2 teaspoon / 4g. (yes)
Olive oil 2 table spoons / 6g. (little)
Ginger fresh 1/2 teaspoon / 4g. (little)
Water 3 cups / 200g. (yes)
Soy Tofu 5/8 lbs - 8oz / 250g. (little)

Cooking instructions:
Cut tofu cubes and marinate with olive oil, tamari, crushed coriander and ginger. Leave at least 1 hour.

Cook Basmati rice with the water. You can season with onion and cardamom.
Roast zucchini and tofu in pan in the hot oil for approx. 5-7 min.
Serve rice and tofu on a plate.
Add the parsley.

Can also be used as a salad for the home and on the go.

9.7   Bath with lavender

Calming, regenerates the central nervous system. Good to fight sleep disorders, loss of appetite and nervous intestinal complaints.

Cooking time approx. 10 min
Calories p. portion: 0
2 portions
Allergens: -

Quantity of ingredients
Lavender blossoms 1 sachet / 5g. (yes)

Instructions:
Put a tied bag with the lavender in the water and let it soak for 10 minutes. The bag can be squeezed several times before removing it.

9.8 Blueberry puree

Bilberry is laxative. Clove dissolves stagnation. Cinnamon powder heats stomach and spleen, improves blood circulation.

Cooking time approx. 10 min
Calories p. portion: 10
1 portions
Allergens: -

Quantity of ingredients
Blueberry 1/2 oz / 20g. (yes)
Clove 1 piece / 1g. (yes)
Water 1 cup / 250g. (yes)
Cinnamon ground 1 pinch / 0,1g. (yes)

Cooking instructions:
Boil blueberries with cinnamon and clove in water for 10 minutes. Remove the cinnamon and clove. Puree. Sweet as desired.

9.9 Buddhist reissue soup

Little laxative. Good to fight blood circulation disorders, risk of embolism, high blood pressure, a headache, heart attack and stroke.

Cooking time approx. 2-4 hours
Calories p. portion: 280
2 portions
Allergens: G

Quantity of ingredients
Butter Bio 1 table spoon / 10g. (yes)
Cow's milk (1.5% fat) 1 cup / 120g. (yes)
Honey 1 teaspoon / 3g. (little)
Water 3 cups / 350g. (yes)
Rice variety any 1 cup / 120g. (yes)

Cooking instructions:
Bring the rice to boil soft in the water for for 2 to 4 hours. At the end of the cooking time add some milk, honey and butter.
This basic recipe can be expanded as desired (sweet, salty). The indicated quantity is sufficient for 4 days (keep in a refrigerator)

Variant: The taste can be refined with cinnamon or vanilla.

9.10 Carrot and rice gruel soup

Stops diarrhea, good to fight fever, strengthens immune system, reduces blood pressure.

Cooking time approx. 10 min
Calories p. portion: 101
1 portions
Allergens: -

Quantity of ingredients
Salt 1 teaspoon / 4g. (little)
Basic recipe for a rice soup (Congee) 1 cup / 120g. (recommended)
Carrot 2 pieces / 100g. (recommended)

Cooking instructions:
Peel and grate carrots. Heat the rice soup (according to the basic recipe) till it boils and add the grated carrots and salt.
Cook for 10 minutes.

9.11 Carrots with potato foam - Also for babies from 8 months

Promotes spleen and liver, reduces blood pressure, strengthens immune system. Improves digestion, regenerates skin, supports urination, lowers cholesterol, promotes the production of stool and urine, strengthens blood, strengthens nerves.

Cooking time approx. 30 min
Calories p. portion: 316
1 portions
Allergens: G

Quantity of ingredients
Butter Bio 1 table spoon / 10g. (yes)
Potato (mealy) 1/4 lbs - 4oz / 100g. (recommended)
Pork meat 1/8 lbs - 2oz / 40g. (little)
Carrot (Early Carrot) 3/8 lbs - 6oz / 150g. (recommended)

Anise (Common Fennel) 1 pinch / 0,2g. (recommended)
Water 2 table spoons / 20g. (yes)
Honey 1/2 teaspoon / 2g. (little)

Cooking instructions:
Clean the carrots, wash thoroughly, peel thinly and cut into thin slices.
Cut the meat into strips.
Wash the potatoes, cook in a small saucepan with little water in about 15 minutes.
Melt half of the butter in a saucepan, fry the carrots and the meat in it. If necessary, add 2-3 tablespoons of water, put the lid on and cook everything over low heat in about 15 minutes.
Add the honey, the anise and the remaining butter and remove the pot from the heat.
Peel the potatoes and press directly onto the plate with the potato press. Distribute the honey carrots over it.

9.12 Chicken soup with egg yolk and parsley

Strengthens blood, strengthens bone marrow, reduces blood pressure, strengthens immune system. Parsley stimulates liver function, harmonizes liver and spleen, strengthens eyesight, detoxifying.

Cooking time approx. 10 min
Calories p. portion: 118
2 portions
Allergens: CL

Quantity of ingredients
Parsley 1 table spoon / 10g. (recommended)
Chicken yolk 1 piece / 10g. (little)
Basic recipe for a chicken soup (warming) 2 cup / 500g. (recommended)

Cooking instructions:
Cook the chicken broth according to the basic recipe.
Heat broth and bubble the egg yolk. Sprinkle the chopped parsley over it and let it rest for about 2 minutes. Drink in small sips.

9.13 Corn coffee with cardamom

Diuretic, forcing spleen, supports urination, relaxes, reduces fat.

Cooking time approx. 5 min
Calories p. portion: 3
1 portions
Allergens: -

Quantity of ingredients
Water 1 cup / 120g. (yes)
Cereal coffee 1 table spoon / 15g. (yes)
Cardamom 2 cores / 1g. (yes)

Cooking instructions:
Boil water, coffee, sugar and cardamom. Let it set for one min before drinking.

9.14 Cottage cheese with steamed fruit

Good to fight loss of appetite, promotes digestion, supports urination.

Cooking time approx. 20 min
Calories p. portion: 214
2 portions
Allergens: G

Quantity of ingredients
Cottage cheese 3/4 lbs / 300g. (recommended)
Apple (sour) 1 piece / 100g. (little)
Pear 1 piece / 100g. (little)

Cooking instructions:
Wash apples and pears well, do not peel, and chop small. In a pot with steam filter, boil them al dente, remove and allow to cool down.
Serve the cheese, spread the fruit on it.

9.15 Cranberry yogurt mix

Good to fight acute or chronic constipation of the intestine, oral mucosal inflammation, diarrhea, flatulence, throat irritation.

Cooking time approx. 5 min
Calories p. portion: 57
2 portions
Allergens: GO

Quantity of ingredients
Mineral water 1 cup / 250g. (little)
Cranberry jam 2 table spoons / 20g. (yes)
Yogurt (natural, 1.5% fat) 1/4 lbs - 4oz / 125g. (yes)

Cooking instructions:
Mix yoghurt, cranberry jam and mineral water until frothy.

9.16 Cucumber soup

Diuretic, detoxifying, suppresses conversion of sugar into fat, lowers cholesterol, prevents cancer, promotes digestion, diaphoretic, dries out, good to fight yeast infections.

Cooking time approx. 20 min
Calories p. portion: 96
4 portions
Allergens: M

Quantity of ingredients
Water 2 cup / 500g. (yes)
Sage 3 leaves / 3g. (yes)
Cardamom 1 pinch / 1g. (yes)
Olive oil 2 table spoons / 35g. (little)
Cucumber 2 pieces / 400g. (little)
Coriander 1 pinch / 1g. (yes)
Mustard 1/2 teaspoon / 0,5g. (little)
Salt 1 pinch / 1g. (little)

Cooking instructions:
Heat oil and roast short the small cucumbers. Add Mustard seeds, coriander, cardamom and salt. Add water. Simmer for 10-15 min. Puree and decorate with fresh chopped sage.

9.17 Curdcheesedumplings on strawberry pulp

Strawberry forcing spleen and stomach, strengthens blood. Chicken egg calms nerves and stomach.

Cooking time approx. 30 min
Calories p. portion: 553
5 portions
Allergens: ACG

Quantity of ingredients
Salt 1 pinch / 1g. (little)
Sugar - icing sugar 2 table spoons / 20g. (little)
Chicken egg 2 pieces / 120g. (little)
Butter Bio 1/8 lbs - 2oz / 40g. (yes)
Spelled semolina 3/8 lbs - 6oz / 150g. (yes)
Curd cheese 20% 1,1 lbs / 500g. (yes)
Breadcrumbs (wheat bread, bread roll) 2 table spoons / 25g. (yes)
Butter Bio 1/4 lbs - 4oz / 100g. (yes)
Strawberries 1,1 lbs / 500g. (yes)
Sugar - icing sugar 2 table spoons / 25g. (little)

Cooking instructions:
Curdcheese, grit, butter, eggs, powdered sugar and salt to a smooth dough. Keep the dough 15 mins in the refrigiator to settle down. Then shape small dumplings with a diameter of approx 4cm and boil them for about 10 minutes in slightly boiling salt water. Heat butter in a pan and roast the breadcrumbs golden brown. Roll the dumplings carefully into the crumbs.
Serve the dumplings with the strawberry.

9.18 Frozen pineapple juice

Pineapple reduce inflammation, supports urination, cleans the skin.

Cooking time approx. 1 1/2 hours
Calories p. portion: 29
1 portions
Allergens: -

Quantity of ingredients
Pineapple 1/8 lbs - 2oz / 50g. (little)

Cooking instructions:
Juice pineapple yourself or freeze the organic pineapple juice in small portions and if necessary suck.

9.19 Hot water with grape juice

Calms stomach, strengthens tendons and bones, supports urination, promotes digestion.

Cooking time approx. 5 min
Calories p. portion: 87
1 portions
Allergens: -

Quantity of ingredients
Grape juice red 1 cup / 120g. (little)
Water 1/2 cup / 60g. (yes)

Cooking instructions:
Heat the water till it boils and add it to the grape juice.

9.20 Mango banana yoghurt drink ice cold

Good to fight loss of appetite, oral mucosa inflammation. Regulates gastrointestinal function, chronic constipation. Prevents cancer. Diuretic, forcing spleen.

Cooking time approx. 5 min
Calories p. portion: 121
2 portions
Allergens: G

Quantity of ingredients
Mango juice 1/2 cup / 100g. (little)
Acerola fruit nectar or powder 1 teaspoon / 2g. (little)
Banana 1/2 piece / 150g. (recommended)
Yogurt (natural, 1.5% fat) 1/4 lbs - 4oz / 100g. (yes)
Mineral water 1/2 cup / 100g. (little)

Cooking instructions:
Mix all the ingredients and 2-3 ice cubes in a blender.

9.21 Melanzani with olive oil and turmeric

Improves blood circulation, reduces inflammation, relieves pain, promotes digestion, helps to digest fat, supports urination, reduces blood pressure.

Cooking time approx. 30 min
Calories p. portion: 432
2 portions
Allergens: A

Quantity of ingredients
Turmeric (yellow root) 1/2 teaspoon / 1g. (yes)
Aubergine 2 pieces / 300g. (recommended)
Ground 1 pinch / 1g. (recommended)
Tomato 4 pieces / 200g. (little)
Salt 1 pinch / 1g. (little)
White bread (wheat bread) 4 slices / 80g. (yes)
Olive oil 4 table spoons / 60g. (little)

Cooking instructions:
Cut the Melanzani into slices and spread them with the tomatoes on a baking tray. Sprinkle with olive oil and then with turmeric, caraway and salt. Bake them in the tube 20 min.
Serve with the white bread.

9.22 Noodles with turkeymeat and pineapple

Solves bile-, kidney- and bladder stones, provides Vitamin C, strengthens blood, strengthens bone marrow, reduces inflammation, supports urination.

Cooking time approx. 45 min
Calories p. portion: 292
4 portions
Allergens: ACGL

Quantity of ingredients
Curry 3 teaspoons / 6g. ()
Pineapple 5/8 oz / 200g. (little)
Water 1/2 cup / 50g. (yes)
Rapeseed oil 1 table spoon / 12g. (little)

Basic recipe for a vegetable soup (nutritious) 1/2 cup / 100g. (recommended)
Salt 1 pinch / 1g. (little)
Fresh cheese 0,2 lbs / 75g. (little)
Pomegranate 1 piece / 300g. (yes)
Pepper (ground) 1 pinch / 0,5g. ()
Coconut flakes 1 table spoon / 6g. (little)
Noodles (whole grain) with egg 5/8 oz / 200g. (yes)
Turkey breast meat 5/8 oz / 200g. (little)
Cow's milk (whole milk 3.5% fat) 2/3 cup / 180g. (little)
Garlic 1 piece / 2g. ()

Cooking instructions:
Cook the noodles in salt water. Cut the pineapple into cubes and leave for 5 min. to simmer in water. Cut the meat sliced in strips and roast them in the oil. Add the chopped garlic and the pineapple sliced. Add about 50 ml of the pineapple juice and stir in the vegetable broth. Add the milk and the fresh cheese, then stir well until the fresh cheese is completely dissolved.
Now add the curry and simmer for a few minutes until a creamy consistency is reached. Season with salt and pepper.
Now add the noodles in the finished sauce. Cut the pomegranate and release the seeds. Distribute as many kernels on the dressed noodles. Whoever likes it can spread coconut chips over it.

9.23 Olive oil with lemon juice

Good to fight acute constipation.

Cooking time approx. 1 min
Calories p. portion: 93
1 portions
Allergens: -

Quantity of ingredients
Lemon juice 1 teaspoon / 4g. (little)
Olive oil 1 table spoon / 10g. (little)

Cooking instructions:
In case of acute constipation take 1 tablespoon of olive oil with lemon juice in the morning on an empty stomach.

9.24 Oven potatoes with celery-curd cheese (quark)

Promotes spleen, reduces Inflammation, improves digestion, regenerates skin, supports urination, lowers cholesterol.

Cooking time approx. 30 min
Calories p. portion: 304
2 portions
Allergens: GL

Quantity of ingredients
Potato 6 pieces / 400g. (recommended)
Ground caraway 1 pinch / 0,2g. (recommended)
Basic recipe for a vegetable soup (nutritious) 1/2 cup / 100g. (recommended)
Celery root 3 oz / 80g. (recommended)
Salt 1 pinch / 1g. (little)
Pepper (ground) 1 pinch / 0,2g. ()
Lemon juice 1 teaspoon / 3g. (little)
Creme fraiche cheese 1/2 teaspoon / 5g. (little)
Olive oil 2 teaspoons / 5g. (little)
Salt 1 pinch / 1g. (little)
Curd cheese 20% 5/8 oz / 200g. (yes)
Lemon peel 1/2 teaspoon / 1g. (yes)

Cooking instructions:
Celery-curd cheese:
Mix celery with vegetable broth according to basic recipe, caraway and lemon peel. Cook for about 8 minutes until the celery is soft and the vegetable broth almost evaporated. Mix the celery vegetable broth with the lemon juice, finely, and stir until smooth. Season with salt and pepper.

Baked potatoes:
Preheat oven to 200 °C / 400 °F.
Brush the potatoes well, halve them, and place them on a baking tray with the cut surface facing up. Lightly salt the surfaces and sprinkle with oil. Fry the potatoes in the oven for about 25 minutes.
Serve the celery plug to the potatoes.

9.25 Pear compote

Promotes digestion, supports urination.

Cooking time approx. 20 min
Calories p. portion: 100
3 portions
Allergens: -

Quantity of ingredients
Pear 4 / 500g. (little)
Water 1 1/2 cups / 240g. (yes)

Cooking instructions:
Halve organic pears. Cores and skin can be used. Pear in the pot and add water. Simmer for up to 20 minutes until pears are tender.

9.26 Pear juice

Promotes digestion, supports urination.

Cooking time approx. 5 min
Calories p. portion: 180
2 portions
Allergens: -

Quantity of ingredients
Pear 3 pieces / 600g. (little)

Cooking instructions:
Peel pears thinly (vitamins under the skin) and core. Juice in the juicer.

9.27 Polenta with peach

Relieves fatigue, forcing spleen, diuretic, strengthens the defense, good to fight fungi infections, lets urine and bile juice flow, prevents the aging process, strengthens brain cells.

Cooking time approx. 20 min
Calories p. portion: 197

3 portions
Allergens: -

Quantity of ingredients
Vanilla pod 1 pinch / 1g. (yes)
Cinnamon ground 1 pinch / 1g. (yes)
Corn Grease (Polenta) 1 cup / 120g. (yes)
Chili (pod or ground) 1 pinch / 0,1g. ()
Water 1 1/2 cups / 240g. (yes)
Peaches 2-3 pieces / 400g. (little)

Cooking instructions:
Pour the polenta into a pan of hot water with constant stirring until the polenta has the desired consistency. Pull the polenta
 from the fire and let it soak for 10 minutes.

Wash fresh peaches and cut into quarters. Pour into the finished polenta the peaches, add the vanilla and add Chili to taste, stir and let it go for 3 minutes.

Winter varieties: Pickled fruit, pear, apples

9.28 Potato pancakes

Promotes spleen, reduces inflammation, improves digestion, regenerates skin, supports urination, calms nerves and stomach, laxative, antiparasitic.

Cooking time approx. 15 min
Calories p. portion: 893
1 portions
Allergens: ACG

Quantity of ingredients
Rapeseed oil 2 table spoons / 20g. (little)
Herbs various 1 table spoon / 10g. (yes)
Potato (mealy) 5/8 lbs - 8oz / 250g. (recommended)
Salt 1 pinch / 1g. (little)
Cream sour 20% 1/8 lbs - 2oz / 50g. (little)
Chicken egg 1 piece / 35g. (little)
Salt 1 pinch / 1g. (little)
Wheat flour 1/2 oz / 10g. (yes)

Cooking instructions:
Grater the peeled potatoes finely, add the remaining ingredients, mix well and salt. Heat the oil and add small flat cakes to the pan with the spoon. Roast the potato pancakes on both sides crispy golden brown. Place them on the plate with sour cream, salt and sprinkle with herbs.

9.29 Pumpkin soup

Promotes digestion, forcing spleen and stomach, reduces blood pressure, strengthens immune system, prevents cancer, reduces radiation damage, improves digestion, regenerates skin, lowers cholesterol, reduces blood glucose, protects liver.

Cooking time approx. 1 hour
Calories p. portion: 105
3 portions
Allergens: -

Quantity of ingredients
Salt 1 pinch / 1g. (little)
Potato 2 pieces / 120g. (recommended)
Water 1 cup / 120g. (yes)
Onion white 1 piece / 50g. ()
Carrot 2 pieces / 100g. (recommended)
Anise (Common Fennel) 1 pinch / 1g. (recommended)
Pumpkin 3/4 lbs / 300g. (recommended)
Olive oil 1 table spoon / 10g. (little)
Parsley 1 table spoon / 7g. (recommended)

Cooking instructions:
Add the olive oil to the pan, add the diced pumpkin, diced carrots and potatoes. Roast them shortly, add the finely chopped onion, fill with water, add enough water to cover the vegetables at least 3 finger-widths. Boil at low heat.

Season with sea salt, add small cutted parsley, a pinch of anise (little).

Allow to simmer for about 35 minutes. Then purée the soup and add some water, depending on the consistency of the soup.

9.30 Puréed banana

Eat 2 times a day, regulates gastrointestinal function.

Cooking time approx. 7 min
Calories p. portion: 144
1 portions
Allergens: -

Quantity of ingredients
Banana 1 piece / 150g. (recommended)

Cooking instructions:
Mix the banana with the fork or purée with a blender. Leave to brown for at least 5 minutes.

9.31 Rice dulse soup

Promotes spleen and liver, reduces blood pressure, strengthens immune system. Good to fight blood circulation disorders, diarrhea, free radicals. Antipyretic. Vitamin C rich. Promotes the exchange of iron and calcium. Increases resistance to infectious diseases.

Cooking time approx. 5 min
Calories p. portion: 190
2 portions
Allergens: L

Quantity of ingredients
Basic recipe for a rice soup (Congee) 4 cups / 500g. (recommended)
Basic recipe for a vegetable soup (nutritious) 2 cup / 500g. (recommended)
Dulse (seaweed) 2 table spoons / 15g. (yes)

Cooking instructions:
Worm up a portion of pre-cooked basic recipe for a ricesoupe (congee) and a portion pre-cooked basic recipe for a vegetable soup.
Bake the dulse in the oven at 220 degrees for 3 minutes. Spread the crisp dulse over the rice.

9.32 Rice with parsnips

Rich in vitamins, minerals potassium and zinc. Good to fight blood circulation disorders, thrombose, risk of embolism, high blood pressure, a headache, heart attack and stroke, yeast infections.

Cooking time approx. 45 min
Calories p. portion: 206
3 portions
Allergens: -

Quantity of ingredients
Olive oil 1 table spoon / 10g. (little)
Rice variety any 1 cup / 120g. (yes)
Parsnip 3-4 pieces / 450g. (yes)
Water 1 1/2 cups / 200g. (yes)
Sage 1 teaspoon / 3g. (yes)
Salt 1 pinch / 1g. (little)

Cooking instructions:
Peel the parsnips and cut into slices. Fry for a short time in oil. Add the rice and fry again for a short time. Add the water and cook it at least 30 min. Sprinkle with fresh chopped sage.

9.33 Rosemary Potatoes

Reduces Inflammation, improves digestion, regenerates skin, supports urination, lowers cholesterol. Rosemary stimulates digestion, strengthens lung, promotes spleen and kidney, dries out.

Cooking time approx. 30 min
Calories p. portion: 188
2 portions
Allergens: -

Quantity of ingredients
Rosemary 1 teaspoon / 2g. (yes)
Olive oil 1 table spoon / 10g. (little)
Salt (herbal) 1 pinch / 1g. (little)
Potato 6-8 pieces / 420g. (recommended)

Cooking instructions:
Cut the potatoes into halfs, apply a little olive oil on the cut surface, then salt, sprinkle 2 - 3 rosemary needles on the potatoes.
Place the potatoes on the baking tray and bake them in the preheated oven for approx. 25 minutes to 190°C/374°F.

9.34 Semolina porridge with banana

Regulates gastrointestinal function, reduces inflammation, antiallergic, good to fight blood circulation disorders.

Cooking time approx. 15 min
Calories p. portion: 307
1 portions
Allergens: AG

Quantity of ingredients
Banana 1/2 piece / 50g. (recommended)
Butter Bio 1 teaspoon / 4g. (yes)
Spelled semolina 2 table spoons / 30g. (yes)
Cow's milk (whole milk 3.5% fat) 3/4 cup - 6 oz / 200g. (little)

Cooking instructions:
Heat the half of the milk in a small pot. Add the semolina and boil it shortly in the milk. Let it swell at low heat for 3 minutes with constant stirring. Remove the pot from the heat, add the remaining milk with the snow bean and place the mush in a small bowl. Add the butter and the battered banana.
For adults, a pinch of cinnamon can be spread over it.

9.35 Spelled-grid porridge with berries of the season

Little laxative, strengthens immune system, activated cell metabolism, reduces inflammation. Has a stabilizing effect on the blood circulation, good to fight blood circulation disorders.

Cooking time approx. 15 min
Calories p. portion: 244
2 portions
Allergens: AGH

Quantity of ingredients
Water 1/2 cup / 125g. (yes)
Spelled semolina 5 table spoons / 50g. (yes)
Butter Bio 2 teaspoons / 20g. (yes)
Berries of the season 1/4 lbs - 4oz / 100g. (yes)
Honey 1-2 teaspoons / 5g. (little)
Almond 1-2 teaspoons / 5g. (yes)
Peppermint 3-4 leaves / 2g. (yes)
Cow's milk (1.5% fat) 1/2 cup / 125g. (yes)
Cocoa 1 pinch / 0,5g. (little)
Vanilla 1 pinch / 0,2g. (yes)
Cinnamon ground 1 pinch / 0,5g. (yes)
Coconut grated 1 table spoon / 10g. (little)

Cooking instructions:
Stir in spelled semolina in cold water and boil slowly over medium heat.
After boiling, remove from the heat and let simmer for a few minutes.
Depending on the desired consistency, some water may have to be
added. Stir in the butter and fine grated nuts in the mash and
raspberries. Serve with honey or whole-grain sugar as desired.
Spices and aromas: fresh mint, cinnamon or vanilla, cocoa, coconut

Summer: raspberries, blueberries, strawberries

9.36 Spring vegetables - also for babies from the 8th month

Diuretic, supports urination, supports digestion. Diuretic, harmonizes
the stomach and intestines, conducts bowel winds, strengthens immune
system.

Cooking time approx. 1 1/2 hour
Calories p. portion: 64
8 portions
Allergens: G

Quantity of ingredients
Water 1/2 cup / 125g. (yes)
Carrot 1,1 lbs / 500g. (recommended)
Kohlrabi 1,1 lbs / 500g. (yes)
Butter Bio 2 table spoons / 20g. (yes)

Cooking instructions:
Wash the vegetables thoroughly. Clean and peel carrots and turnip cabbage. From the turnip cabbage, finely chop some delicate leaves and set aside. Rasp the carrots and the turnip cabbage. Melt the butter, add the water and the vegetables and cook over medium heat for about 30 minutes. Stir occasionally. Spread the vegetables and cooked water to about 8 deep-frozen bags to a100-150 g (depending on the age of the child). Close the bags, allow them to cool down and freeze them for max 3 months.
If necessary thaw, boil and mix with 80g of boiled potatoes and an egg. (The recipe can easily be varied if you want to use cauliflower, peas or zucchini)

9.37 Tea from anise

Anise (wild fennel) promotes digestion, forcing spleen and stomach.

Cooking time approx. 15 min
Calories p. portion: 3
4 portions
Allergens: -

Quantity of ingredients
Water 2 cup / 500g. (yes)
Anise (Common Fennel) 1 teaspoon / 3g. (recommended)

Cooking instructions:
Heat the water till it boils and put it aside. Add anise.
10 min. to let go.
Pour through a tea strainer. Sweet to taste with honey.

In order to achieve a salutary effect, you should drink 2 cups of anise tea per day.

9.38 Tea from coriander

Coriander promotes digestion, diaphoretic.

Cooking time approx. 10 min
Calories p. portion: 2
4 portions
Allergens: -

Quantity of ingredients
Water 2 cup / 500g. (yes)
Coriander 1 teaspoon / 3g. (yes)

Cooking instructions:
Heat the water till it boils and put it aside. Add coriander and 10 min. to let go. Sweet to taste with honey. Strain when pouring.

9.39 Tea from elderberry blossom tea

Good, if you have a sore throat. Good to fight colds. Promotes urination, good to fight flu, urinary stones, concentration weakness, blackheads, hay fever, rheumatism. Strengthen the immune system, diaphoretic.

Cooking time approx. 10 min
Calories p. portion: 7
4 portions
Allergens: -

Quantity of ingredients
Water 2 cup / 500g. (yes)
Elderberry blossom tee 4 teaspoons / 12g. (recommended)

Cooking instructions:
Heat the water till it boils and put it aside. Add holligan flowers and 10 min. to let go. Sweet to taste with honey. Strain when pouring.

9.40 Tea from fennel

Harmonizes stomach, less bloating.

Cooking time approx. 10 min
Calories p. portion: 0
4 portions
Allergens: -

Quantity of ingredients
Water 2 cup / 500g. (yes)
Fennel tea 2 table spoons / 20g. (recommended)

Cooking instructions:
Heat the water till it boils and put it aside. Add fennel tea and 10 min. to let go. Sweet to taste with honey. Strain when pouring.

9.41 Tea from ginger with honey

Honey relieves pain, detoxifying, bactericide.
Fresh ginger encourages digestion, detoxifying, strengthens bodily production, promotes perspiration, reduces blood lipids, stimulates, dissolves stagnation.

Cooking time approx. 30 min
Calories p. portion: 5
4 portions
Allergens: -

Quantity of ingredients
Honey 2 teaspoons / 6g. (little)
Ginger fresh 1 teaspoon / 3g. (little)
Water 2 cup / 500g. (yes)

Cooking instructions:
Heat the water till it boils and put it aside. Add ginger and 20-30 min. to let go. Sweet to taste with honey.

9.42 Tea from ground

Cumin promotes digestion, reduces flatulence.

Cooking time approx. 10 min
Calories p. portion: 2
4 portions
Allergens: -

Quantity of ingredients
Water 2 cup / 500g. (yes)
Ground 1 teaspoon / 3g. (recommended)

Cooking instructions:
Heat the water till it boils and put it aside. Add crushed cumin and leave for 10 min. to let go. Sweet to taste with honey.
Strain when pouring.

Drink 1 cup 2 times a day.

9.43 Tea from marjoram

Promotes the digestion of fatty foods. Diuretic effect. Antibacterial effect in the climacteric period. Good to fight menopausal complaints.

Cooking time approx. 10 min
Calories p. portion: 0
4 portions
Allergens: -

Quantity of ingredients
Marjoram 2 teaspoons / 6g. (yes)
Water 2 cup / 500g. (yes)

Cooking instructions:
Heat the water till it boils and put it aside. Add marjoram and 10 min. to let go. Sweet to taste with honey. Strain when pouring.

9.44 Tea stomach tea

Promotes digestion.

Cooking time approx. 15 min
Calories p. portion: 3
2 portions
Allergens: -

Quantity of ingredients
Fennel seeds ground 1 teaspoon / 2g. (recommended)
Water 1 cup / 250g. (yes)
Licorice root tea 2 pieces / 3g. (yes)

Cooking instructions:
Put fennel seeds lightly pounded into a kettle with the licorice. Boil
water for about 2 minutes and pour into the kettle. Leave for 10 min and
strain.
(For baby's cool down hand warm and put it in a bottle).

9.45 Tomato with mozzarella

Promotes digestion, helps to digest fat, supports urination, reduces
blood pressure. Affects anorexia, good to fight flatulence, inflammatory
bowel disease, bloating and nausea. Relaxing and reassuring.

Cooking time approx. 5 min
Calories p. portion: 436
1 portions
Allergens: AG

Quantity of ingredients
White bread (wheat bread) 2 slices / 40g. (yes)
Olive oil 2 table spoons / 20g. (little)
Mozzarella 1 piece / 50g. (little)
Salt 1 pinch / 1g. (little)
Tomato 2 pieces / 100g. (little)
Basil (fresh) 5 leaves / 6g. (yes)

Cooking instructions:
Cut tomatoes and mozzarella into slices. Serve with salt, basil and olive
oil. Serve with white bread.

9.46 Vanilla pudding

Helps to fight constipation.

Cooking time approx. 10 min
Calories p. portion: 254
2 portions
Allergens: G

Quantity of ingredients
Pudding powder vanilla 1 package / 37g. (yes)
Cow's milk (whole milk 3.5% fat) 2 cups / 500g. (little)
Sugar white 1 table spoon / 12g. (little)

Cooking instructions:
Give 3-5 tablespoons of milk into a cup, bring the rest in a pot to boil.
Pour the powdered pudding into the cup and stir until free of lumpy. As
soon as the milk boils, add the mixture and simmer under low heat for
about 3 minutes. Divide into prepared bowls.

9.47 Vegetable juice

Promotes digestion, helps to digest fat, supports urination, reduces
blood pressure, strengthens immune system, prevents cancer, reduces
radiation damage, forcing spleen, is stimulating.

Cooking time approx. 15 min
Calories p. portion: 64
1 portions
Allergens: L

Quantity of ingredients
Acerola fruit nectar or powder 1/2 teaspoon / 1g. (little)
Celery root 1/2 oz / 20g. (recommended)
Carrot 1/4 lbs - 4oz / 100g. (recommended)
Tomato 1/4 lbs - 4oz / 100g. (little)
Garlic 1 piece / 2g. ()
Salt 1 teaspoon / 2g. (little)

Cooking instructions:
Peel all ingredients and use the juicer to make a drink. Stir in the
acerola.

9.48 Vegetable semolina soup

Diuretic, harmonizes the stomach and intestines, conducts bowel winds, reduces blood pressure, lowers cholesterol, detoxifying, good to fight loss of appetite, flatulence, inflammatory bowel disease, heartburn, twelffinger intestinal ulcers. Stimulates digestion, reduces pain.

Cooking time approx. 20 min
Calories p. portion: 199
3 portions
Allergens: AEGL

Quantity of ingredients
Potato 1 piece / 80g. (recommended)
Beans (green, fresh) 1/4 lbs / 100g. (little)
Kohlrabi 1/2 piece / 200g. (yes)
Carrot 1 piece / 120g. (recommended)
Soy sauce 1 teaspoon / 3g. (little)
Lovage 1/2 teaspoon / 2g. (recommended)
Celery root 3/8 lbs - 6oz / 150g. (recommended)
Butter Bio 1 table spoon / 20g. (yes)
Wheat semolina 2 table spoons / 24g. (yes)
Basic recipe for a vegetable soup (nutritious) 2 cup / 500g. (recommended)
Parsnip 1 piece / 180g. (yes)

Cooking instructions:
Worm the prepared vegetable soup; cook the vegetables in the soup softly. Spread some wheatgrass and let it swell. At the end, add lovage-green and a little butter and taste with soy sauce.

10 Effects of food

10.1 Use ingredients: recommendable

Acai powder
Anise (Common Fennel)
Aubergine
Banana
Banana (cooking banana)
Basic recipe for a beef soup
Basic recipe for a beef soup (warming)
Basic recipe for a chicken soup (warming)
Basic recipe for a fish soup
Basic recipe for a rice soup (Congee)
Basic recipe for a vegetable soup (nutritious)
Bitter Herb liqueur
Black caraway
Blackberry's
Blue mallow tee
Cantaloupe
Carrot
Carrot (Early Carrot)
Carrot juice without sugar
Celery root
Chamomile tea
Chervil
Chervil dried
Chinese pearl barley
Codfish
Cottage cheese
Cream 10% coffee cream
Cress
Crucian

Dill
Elderberries
Elderberry blossom tee
Fennel seeds ground
Fennel tea
Fox nut, gorgon nut, makhana
Gourd
Ground
Ground caraway
Herbal tea mix
Hibiscus
Hokkaido pumpkin
Kudzu
Lamb's lettuce
Lily bulbs
Loquate / Japanese medlar
Lotus roots
Lotus seeds
Lovage
Mascarpone cheese
Parsley
Parsley root
Potato
Potato (mealy)
Pumpkin
Red beet
Turnips
Watermelon
Wax gourd
Zucchini

10.2 Use ingredients: yes

Almond
Aloe juice
Amaranth
Amaranth Pops
Angelica root
Apple puree
Arrowroot
Baking powder
Balm
Banchatee (green tea)
barberry
Barley
Barley flour
Barley grass powder
Barley grouts

Barley malt
Barley not peeled
Basil
Basil (fresh)
Batavia
Bay leaf
Berries of the season
Blackberry leaves
Blueberry
Borage
Boxhorn clover seeds
Bread roll
Bread with carob kernel flour
Breadcrumbs (wheat bread, bread roll)
Broccoli

Buckbean
Buckwheat
Buckwheat (roasted) Kasha
Bulgur (cereals)
Burdock root tea
Butter (half fat)
Butter Bio
Buttermilk
Calamari
Carambola (Star fruit)
Cardamom
Carob flour, St. john's bread
Cereal coffee
Chamomile
Channa-Dal
Chicken egg white
Chickweed
Chicory
Chlorella (fresh water)
Chrysanthemum blossom tea
Cinnamon ground
Cinnamon sticks
Clove
Cod
Coix (seeds) YiYi Ren
Compote (fruits of the season)
Coriander
Coriander (fresh)
Corn
Corn (fast polenta)
Corn (roasted)
Corn flour
Corn Grease (Polenta)
Corn silk tea
Corn starch
Couscous
Cow's milk (1.5% fat)
Crab
Cranberry
Cranberry
Cranberry jam
Cranberry juice
Cream sour 10%
Creamer
Crispbread
Cumin (Caraway seed)
Curcuma
Curd cheese 20%
Currant (black)
Currant (red)
Currant (white)
Daisy
Dandelion (young plants)
Dandelion juice

Dandelionroots tea
Dashi
Dulse (seaweed)
Endive salad
Fenugreek (Trigonella foenum-graecum)
Feta cheese
Fig
Fish pieces mixed (fresh water)
Flounder
Flower pollen
Freshwater crab
Freshwater fish
Fruit tea
Galangal
Gelatin white
Gelee Royal
Gentian root
Gentian root tea
Ginkgo fruit
Ginseng
Ginseng root
Goat and sheep's milk
Goat cheese
Gooseberry
Green tea
Guava
Halibut (Flatfish)
Hawthorn
Herbs bitter
Herbs of Provence
Herbs various
Herbs wild
Hibiscus tea
Hijiki
Hyssop
Iceberg lettuce
Jasmine blossoms tee
Jellyfish
Juniper berry
Kalmus
Kefir
King Solomon's-seal
Kohlrabi
Kukicha tea
Kumquats
Ladyfingers
Lamb's lettuce
Lavender blossoms
Leaf salads (bitter)
Lemon Balm (dried)
Lemon Balm (fresh)
Lemon peel
Lemongrass

Lettuce
Licorice root tea
Lime blossom tea
Liver smoothing tea
Lobster
Longane
Lovage seeds
Luo Han Guo fruit
Lychee
Lychee In Preserved
Lye roll
Mallow (Malva sylvestris) blossom tea
Mare's milk
Marjoram
Mediterranean fish (cod, plaice, haddock, sea eel, mackerel)
Medlar
Millet
Millet flakes
Miso
Miso black (fermented)
Mulberry fruit
Mulled Wine Spice
Mullet
Mussels
Nasturtium (nose-twister or nose-tweaker)
Nettles
Noodles (wheat) with egg
Noodles (wheat, lasagne) with egg
Noodles (wheat, ribbon noodles) with egg
Noodles (wheat, spaghetti) with egg
Noodles (whole grain) with egg
Nori, purple seaweed, red algae
Nutmeg
Oat
Oat flakes (whole grain)
Oat flour
Oat fusion (baby food)
Oat milk
Octopus
Octopus
Okra
Orange blossom
Oregano dried
Oregano fresh
Oysters
Papaya
Parsnip
Passion blssoms tea
Passion fruit
Pearl barley
Pearl barley

Peppermint
Peppermint tea
Perch
Pimento
Plaice
Pomegranate
Potato flour
Prickly pear
Processed cheese 12%
Pudding powder vanilla
Quince
Quinoa
Radicchio
Radish black
Radish leaves
Raspberry
Raspberry leaf tea
Red berry (without sugar)
Ribworttea
Rice (fragrance)
Rice (Gaoliang / Sorghum)
Rice (whole grain)
Rice Basmati
Rice flour
Rice long grain rice
Rice malt
Rice mash
Rice noodles
Rice red
Rice round grain
Rice starch
Rice sticky
Rice sweet
Rice variety any
Romaine lettuce / lettuce salad
Rose blossom tea
Rose hip
Rose hip tea
Rose leaf tea
Rosefish
Rosemary
Rucola
Rusk
Rye
Rye flour
Safflower (Dyer's thistle / Hong Hua)
Saffron
Sage
Sago (cereals)
Salmon
Sea buckthorn
Seacrab
Shark
Sheep's milk

Sheep's milk yoghurt
Shrimp
Shrimps
Skim milk powder
Slug
Sorrel
Sour cream 15% fat
Sour milk
Sour milk cheese 20%
Sourdough
Spelled flakes
Spelled semolina
Spiny lobsters
Spurdog (spiny dogfish, Schillerlocken)
Star anise
Stevia (candyleaf, sweetleaf)
Strawberries
Sugar substitute (sweetener)
Suplementary nutrition
Sweet potato
Tarragon (Estragon)
Tea mixture uric acid lowering
Thyme
Thyme dried
Topinambur
Trout
Tsampa (roasted barley flour)
Turmeric (yellow root)
Turnip
Valerian
Vanilla

Vanilla pod
Vanilla powder
Wakame
Water
Water hot
Wheat
Wheat bulgur
Wheat flakes
Wheat flatbread/pita bread
Wheat flour
Wheat semolina
Wheat semolina for children
Wheatgrass juice
Wheatgrass powder
Whey
White bread (baguette)
White bread (pretzel sticks)
White bread (roll)
White bread (wheat bread)
White breadcrumbs
White dumpling bread (wheat bread cut into chunks)
Whitefish
Wild herbs
Wild strawberries
Wormwood herb
Yam root, yam root tuber
Yarrow
Yarrow tea
Yogi tea
Yogurt (natural, 1.5% fat)

10.3 Use ingredients: little

Acerola fruit nectar or powder
Agar agar (kelp)
Agave nectar
Apple (sour)
Apple (sweet)
Apple juice (natural cloudy)
Apricot jam
Avocado
Bean oil
Beans (green, fresh)
Bearberry leaf
Beef fillet
Beef meat
Beef meat (calf)
Beef meatbones
Beef Oxtail pieces
Beef soup meat
Berry juice
Blackberry jam

Blueberry dried
Blueberry jam
Blueberry juice
Borage oil
Buckwheat whole grain
Capers in olive oil
Cauliflower
Caviar
Champignon
Chestnut puree
Chestnuts
Chicken egg
Chicken meat
Chicken yolk
Clarified butter
Cocoa
Coconut flakes
Coconut grated
Cooking oil

Corn germ oil
Cow's milk (whole milk 3.5% fat)
Cranberries
Cream sour 20%
Creme fraiche cheese
Cucumber
Cucumber (bitter)
Cucumber (spicy cucumber)
Curd cheese 40%
Currant jam (black)
Currant jam (red)
Currant juice (black)
Currants (black)
Currants (red)
Dates dried
Dates red
Deer meat
Deer meat
Deer's Bones
Ducks egg
Edam cheese
Feta cheese
Fig dried
Fish innards
Fish remains
Fish sauce
Fresh cheese
Fresh cheese from soya
Fresh cheese with herbs
Fructose (glucose)
Fruit mix juice
Ginger fresh
Ginger powder
Goat
Goose eg
Gouda cheese
Grape juice red
Grape juice white
Grapes red
Grapes white
Grapeseed oil
Grass carp
Green spelt
Herring
Honey
Hop
Horse meat
Kiwi
Kombu seaweed (Saccharina japonica)
Lamb bones
Lamb meat
Lamb shoulder
Lemon juice
Linseed oil

Mackerel
Malt
Mango
Mango juice
Maple syrup
Margarine
Margarine (diet)
Mineral water
Mold cheese
Mozzarella
Multi-grain bread (gray bread)
Mustard
Mustard seeds
Mutton
Mutton
Nectarine
Oat flakes roasted
Olive oil
Orange jam
Palm oil
Peaches
Peaches (canned)
Peanut oil
Pear
Pear juice
Peppers
Pheasant
Pigeon
Pigeon egg
Pineapple
Pineapple (from a can)
Pineapple juice without sugar
Poppy
Pork ham
Pork ham cooked
Pork ham smoked
Pork knuckle
Pork meat
processed cheese 30%
Pumpkin seed oil
Quail
Quail egg
Rabbit
Rabbit (wild)
Rabbit meat
Raisins
Rapeseed oil
Raspberry dried (immature)
Raspberry jam
Salt
Salt (herbal)
Savory
Sesame oil
Soy flour

Soy noodles
Soy sauce
Soy Tofu
Soy Tofu smoked
Soybean milk
Soybean oil
Spelled (Dark) bread
Spelled grain
Spelled wholemeal flour
St. Benedict's thistle, blessed thistle, holy thistle, spotted thistle
Strawberry jam
Strawberry Juice
Sugar - icing sugar
Sugar brown
Sugar candy white
Sugar cane sugar
Sugar fructose - fruit sugar
Sugar glucose - grapes sugar
Sugar Milk Sugar
Sugar molasses
Sugar palm sugar
Sugar white
Sunflower oil

Thistle oil
Tomato
Tomato juice
Tomato paste
Tomato puree
Tonic Water
Truffle
Tuna
Turkey breast meat
Turkey ham
Umeboshi paste
Vanilla sugar natural
Vegetable juice
Vinegar (Apple vinegar)
Vinegar (Red wine vinegar)
Vinegar Aceto Balsamico
Vinegar Aceto Balsamico white
Walnut oil
Wheat germ oil
Wild boar meat
Yeast
Yoghurt vanilla
Yogurt (natural, 3.5% fat)

10.4 Do not use contra-acting foods

Adzuki beans
Agrimony
Almond marzipan
Almond milk
Almond puree
Anchovy / Sardine
Apricot
Apricot dried
Apricot nectar
Apricots
Apricots juice
Artichoke
Asparagus (green or white)
Bamboo shoots
Basic recipe for a duck soup
Beef bone marrow
Beef heart
Beef heart (calf)
Beef kidney
Beef liver
Beef lungs (calf)
Beef stomach
Beer (alcohol-free)
Beer (alcohol-reduced)
Beer (Pils)
Beer (Top-fermented German dark beer)

Bitter Lemon
Bitter liqueur
Bitter orange peel
Black beans
Black fungus mushroom
Black tea
Blackberry dried (unripe fruit)
Black-eyed peas
Blackthorn (Sloe)
Bocksdorn fruits (Fructus Lycii, Goji, goji berry)
Boletus mushroom
Brazil nuts
Brie cheese
Broad beans (thick beans)
Brown ale
Brussels sprouts
Bush beans
Butter beans white
Camembert
Campari
Carp
Cashews
Celery sticks
Chanterelle
Chard
Chenpi (chinese tangerine bowl)

Cherry
Cherry (sour)
Cherry compote
Cherry juice
Chicken Blood
Chicken heart
Chicken liver
Chicken stomach
Chickpeas
Chili (pod or ground)
Chinese cabbage
Chives
Chocolate
Chocolate (Diabetic)
Clementine
Clementines
Coconut fat
Coconut meat
Coconut milk
Coffee
Cola drink
Cola drink (low calorie)
Cream (30% fat)
Cream sour 30%
Cream, sweet 30%
Curry
Curry paste red
Deer's kidneys
Duck (heart)
Duck (slaughtered)
Dyer's broom herb
Eel
Eel smoked
Emmental cheese
Evening primrose oil
Fennel
Fernet Branca (herbal bitter liqueur)
French beans
Gail plum
Garam Masala powder
Garlic
Ginger oil
Ginseng liqueur
Goat and sheep's blood
Goat and sheep's brain
Goat and sheep's liver
Goat and sheep's stomach
Goose
Goose fat
Goose parts
Gooseblood
Gorgonzola
Grapefruit (Pomelo)
Grapefruit dried peel

Grapefruit juice
Greengage
Hazelnuts
Honey wine (Met)
Horehound leaves
Kaki plum
Kidney beans (red)
Lamb kidneys
Lamb liver
Leek
Lemon
Lentils
Lentils black
Lentils red
Lentils yellow
Lima beans
Lime
Linseed
Linseed (crushed)
Lychee liqueur
Manioc flour
Martini
Mayonnaise 50%
Mayonnaise 80%
Mirabelle plum
Miso paste (soy bean paste)
Mixed Pickels
Morel (black, dried)
Morel, dried
Mu Erh Mushroom
Muesli
Mung bean
Mung bean sprouting
Mustard Dijon
Mustard medium hot
Mustard sweet
Oat meal
Olives
Olives green
Onion (shallot)
Onion (spring onion)
Onion read
Onion white
Orange
Orange dried peel
Orange grated peel
Orange juice
Orange peel
Oyster mushroom
Oyster shell powder
Parmesan
Peanut (roasted)
Peanut butter
Peanuts

Peas
Peas, green
Pepper (ground)
Pepper Cayenne
Pepper powder (hot)
Pepper white (ground)
Peppercorns
Pepperoni
Pepperoni, red, pitted, halved
Pepperoni, yellow, pitted, halved
Peppers (rose peppers)
Peppers (sweet)
Peppers powder
Pickle
Pig blood
Pine nuts
Pinto beans speckled
Pistachios
Plum
Plum dried
Plums
Pork Bacon
Pork brain
Pork fat (lard)
Pork heart
Pork kidneys
Pork Lard
Pork liver
Pork lung
Pork marrow bones
Pork sausage (Bratwurst)
Pork skin
Pork stomach
Pork/beef sausage (smoked)
Pork's intestine
Prosecco
Psyllium seed
Puff pastry
Pumpernickel (dark bread)
Pumpkin seeds
Rabbit liver
Radish
Radish (white, green, purple-red)
Radish horseradish
Red cabbage
Red wine
Reishi mushroom

Rhubarb
Rice black
Rice wild (nature rice)
Rum
Rye wholemeal bread
Sake
Salsify
Sauerkraut (cuted cabbage fermented)
Savoy cabbage / kale
Sea cucumber
Sesame oil roasted
Sesame paste (Tahini)
Sesame, black
Sesame, white
Sherry (whine)
Shiitake, dried
Sour cherries
Soya Cuisine (soy cream)
Soybeans
Soybeans, black
Soybeans, blacks, fermented
Soybeans, yellow
Spinach
Spirit
Sunflower seeds
Tabasco
Tangerine
Toast bread (whole grain)
Tomato dried
Trout (smoked)
Umeboshi plums (Japanese apricots)
Walnuts
Walnuts roasted
Wheat beer
Wheat bran
Wheat flour whole grain
Wheat/Rye/Gray-black bread with yeast
White beans
White cabbage
White wine
Whole grain bread
Wholemeal flour
Wild garlic (garlic spinach)
Wormwood
Yew nut

11 Herbs and their effects

11.1 Basil (fresh)

It has a beneficial effect on flatulence and nausea, relaxing and soothing. Good against amphysema, bronchitis, whooping cough, high blood pressure, headache, mouth odor, warts, hiccup, gout, migraine.

11.2 Savory

Stomach-strengthening, soothing and appetizing. Ideal for prevention against colds, strengthens the immune system. In case of incontinence or nocturnal wetting (not for children), put the beans in liquor for libido.

11.3 Coriander

The essential oils are appetizing, digestive, cramping and soothing in stomach and intestinal disorders.

11.4 Herbs various

Appetizing, lots of trace elements and vitamins

11.5 Lavender blossoms

Calms the central nervous system, relieves anxiety, against sleep disturbances, loss of appetite and nervous intestinal complaints.

11.6 Lovage

Stimulates digestion, reduces pain. Extracts of the root are used to flush out urinary tract infections and prevent kidney gravel.

11.7 Marjoram

Helps to digest fat foods, strengthens digestive organs, helps against colds, strengthens menstruation, promotes skin healing.

11.8 Oregano dried

It has an anti-digestive, calming and nerve-strengthening effect, helps against cramping stomach and intestinal disorders. The ingredient Carvacrol has an anti-inflammatory effect.

11.9 Parsley

Stimulates liver function, detoxifies. Forces urinating. Relieves flatulence. Digestive and menstrual stimulating, birth-accelerating, memory-enhancing, blood-purifying, skin-smoothing.

11.10 Peppermint

Relaxes, frees the lungs and the nose (inhale), regulates the cycle. Stimulates bile flow and bile production, antispasmodic in gastrointestinal disorders, antimicrobial and antiviral.

11.11 Rosemary

Promotes digestion, relieves bloating, strengthens lung, spleen and kidney. Affects the circulation and nerves.
Appetizing. Baths help against circulatory disorders as well as with gout and rheumatism.

11.12 Sage

Against yeast infections. The leaves have a digestive effect and are used in greasy foods. Antiperspirant effect.
Helps to relieve coughing attacks. Dries out (TCM).

11.13 Thyme dried

Disinfecting. It stimulates the blod circulation, increases the appetite and helps to digest fat meat better. Strengthens lungs and spleen (TCM).

11.14 Lemon Balm (fresh)

Stimulating, antibacterial, encouraging, relaxing, antispasmodic, cooling, antipyretic, analgesic, sweat-inducing, virus-inhibiting. Good for colds, fever, flu, cough, bronchitis, asthma, loss of appetite, bloating, heartburn.

12 Basics of Nutrition

The basic principles of nutrition described herein are general recommendations. They are not aimed at a specific form of therapy. Recommendations concerning a therapy have priority.

12.1 Nutrition

Regular meals in a relaxed atmosphere. A warm breakfast is considered a good start into the day.

The main meals ought to be taken for lunch – supper in the early evening. Pay attention to feeling hungry or sated: don't eat too much nor remain hungry is the rule

Prepare the meals freshly from natural, regional products. Frozen, heat-conserved, industrially prepared or foodstuffs cooked in the microwave oven are rejected.

Choice of foodstuffs according to the season: more cooling food in summer, more warming food in winter.

Eat cooked food at least twice a day. Food and drinks ought to be lukewarm, never ice-cold or hot.

Raw vegetables, briefly cooked vegetables, freshly squeezed juices and mineral water are not recommended. Milk and dairy products are only included in the diet if they don't cause problems.

Don't use therapeutic recipes over a longer period without consulting your doctor or therapist.

Varied food
Enjoy the diversity of foodstuffs. Characteristics of a balanced nutrition are variety, suitable combination and a balanced quantity of rich and low energy foodstuffs (on one hand avoiding undersupply with essential nutrients and on the other hand to take to many undesirable substances).

A lot of Cereal Products - and Potatoes
Bread, pasta, rice, cereal flakes (best wholemeal) as well as potatoes contain almost no fat, but many vitamins, mineral nutrients, trace elements, roughage and secondary plant substances. These foodstuffs ought to be taken with low-fat side dishes.

Vegetables and Fruit – „Take Five" every day ...
5 portions of vegetables and fruit a day, as fresh as possible, briefly cooked, or maybe one portion as a juice – ideal as a side dish to every meal as well as snack between meals: Thus a lot of vitamins, mineral nutrients as well as roughage and secondary plant substances

Daily milk and dairy products

Milk and Dairy Products every Day, once or twice per Week Fish; meat, sausages as well as eggs moderately. These foodstuffs contain valuable nutrients like calcium in the milk, iodine selenium and omega-3 fat acids in saltwater fish. Meat is favorable due to its high content of disposable iron and the vitamins B1, B6 and B12. Quantities of 300 – 600 g meat and sausage per week are sufficient. Prefer low-fat products, especially in meat- and dairy products.

Low-fat and fatty Foodstuffs

Fat supplies us with essential fat acids and fatty foodstuffs contain also fat-soluble vitamins. Fat is high in energy; therefore much fat in the food may cause overweight, possibly also cancer. Too many saturated fat acids may further a tendency for cardio-vascular diseases in the long term. Prefer vegetable oils and fats (e.g. rapeseed-, olive-, soya-oils and solid fats produced therefrom). Beware of invisible fat in meat- and dairy products, pastry and sweets as well as in fast-food and convenience foods. 70 – 90 g fat per day is sufficient.

Moderately Sugar and Salt

Take sugar and foods/drinks containing various kinds of sugar (e.g. glucose syrup) only occasionally. Use herbs and spices as well as a little salt creatively. Prefer salt containing iodine.

Plenty of Liquids

Water is absolutely essential. Drink 1-2 l liquids every day. Prefer water (with or without gas) and other low-calorie drinks. Alcoholic drinks should not be taken.

Tasty Dishes, carefully cooked

Cook the meals with as low temperatures and as short as possible, using little water and fat – this preserves the original taste, keeps the nutrients intact and prevents the production of harmful compounds.

Take time and enjoy the food

Take your Time and enjoy your Food
Eating consciously helps to eat right. The eye enjoys food, too. It's fun, invites to enjoy varied dishes and stimulates the feeling of satiety.

Watch your Weight and stay in Motion

A balanced diet and a lot of exercise and sport (30 – 60 min/day) are a healthy combination. The right weight furthers well-being and health. Thermals, directional effectiveness, digestive power

There are various criteria for judging the effectiveness of herbs and foodstuffs.

The use of certain herbs and ingredients is based on observations of the effects on the body which these foodstuffs, herbs and spices show after having eaten them. The medical science has developed following system: Every ingredient or herb has a directional effectiveness. Furthermore, there are herbs which have a special effect on certain organs.

The basic condition for a healthy metabolism is to obtain sufficient energy from food and that the digestive process doesn't use too much energy. An easily digestible meal makes content and sated, doesn't cause flatulence and fatigue after the meal. The perfect spices increase the healthiness of our meals. Very often, just small doses of herbs and spices will suffice. They are not used to make us sated, but to help our digestive organs to digest the food.

12.2 Recipes

The recipes list the ingredients to be used and the cooking instructions show how the dish is prepared. The list of ingredients shows the concerned quantities as well as the relevance for the therapy. If you find „less than mentioned", try to comply or find an alternative from the „list of recommended foodstuffs". Mostly it shall result just in a small change of taste when you simply avoid this ingredient.

Mild cooking methods: boiling, stewing, poaching, steaming
Strong cooking methods: barbecuing, roasting, frying, smoking
Balanced cooking methods: deep-frying, baking brick
Deep-freezing and warming in the microwave oven should be avoided (denaturalization).

12.3 Foodstuffs

Foodstuffs have an effect on body and soul like medicinal herbs, only a very much milder one. Dietary advice is mainly based on regional foodstuffs. The knowledge about the effects of each foodstuff and the knowledge, when which foodstuff shall be used, is based on the orthodox school of medicine. Use ecologic-organic products, if possible. As everything should be cooked for a long time due to a better digestability and very rarely eaten raw, the food agrees with everyone.

The classification of the foodstuffs according to their effect on the body is the basis in order to achieve a harmonious status of health.

Dietary advisors do not recommend certain foodstuffs for everyone. The individual diet is tailor-made for the individual constitution.

Buy only fresh and ripe fruit and vegetables. You ought to leave unripe fruit and vegetables and such with brown spots and wilted leaves behind in the market. In this case take deep-frozen goods (never ready-to-serve dishes!). Fruit and vegetables are deep-frozen immediately after harvesting and often contain more vitamins and minerals than the goods from the vegetable shelf. Whereas conserved or tinned goods contain very much less biological substances. Also, salt, sugar and others are mostly added to the latter. Never leave the foodstuffs in the water after washing them to avoid that many vital substances get drowned. Clean salads, fruit and vegetables immediately before serving.

Please make sure of the hygienic processing of foodstuffs. Clean your salads, fruit and vegetables carefully. When cooking with meat, prepare all ingredients first and then process the meat products. Clean the worktop and tools very carefully. Wooden surfaces ought to be treated with a mild disinfectant regularly in order to reduce germination.

Store fruit and vegetables separately, if possible. Harvested fruit and vegetables are still alive and emit e.g. ethylene gas, which makes other products ripen and age faster. Keep meat and fish in the closed packaging or store them in the fridge in closed containers.

12.4 Herbs

There are some basic rules for storing medicinal herbs. On principle, herbs must be protected from direct sunlight, humidity and heat.

Containers for the storage of herbs may be glasses, ceramic jars and even plastic containers. However, plastic is a rather unsuitable material and should only be a short-term solution. In case of glass containers, use a dark material.

Medicinal herbs cannot be kept for any long period. The shelf life of herbs is limited. However, it can be prolonged with suitable storage. The place should be dark, rather cool and absolutely dry. A wooden medicine cabinet, placed not directly next to a source of heat, would be ideal. Never buy large quantities of herbs so as not to have to throw them away. Label the container with the name of the herb and the date of harvesting or processing.

13 Other dietic-books

The following syndromes of dietetics, TCM or for a therapy supplement for cancer are available.

Dietetics

E001. Nutrition of the infant - baby food
E002. Nutrition during lactation
E003. Nutrition in old age
E004. Nutrition of children and adolescents
E005. Nutrition of athletes
E006. Light weight
E007. Pregnancy
E008. Full food

Protein and electrolyte - kidneys
E009. (hemodialysis) dialysis treatment
E010. Acute renal failure
E011. Chronic renal insufficiency
E012. Nephrotic syndrome
E013. Kidney stones (nephrolithiasis)

Gastrointestinal tract - pancreas
E014. Acute pancreatitis (inflammation of the pancreas)
E015. Chronic pancreatitis (inflammation of the pancreas)

Gastrointestinal tract - small intestine and large intestine
E016. Acute obstipation (constipation)
E017. Chronic obstipation (constipation)
E018. Colon irritabile
E019. Diverticulitis
E020. Acquired lactose intolerance (lactose malabsorption)
E021. Fructose malabsorption
E022. Glutensensitive enteropathy (celiac disease)
E023. Colectomy
E024. Short Bowel Syndrome

Gastrointestinal tract - liver, gallbladder, bile ducts
E025. Acute and chronic hepatitis (inflammation of the liver)
E026. Cholelithiasis (bile stones)
E027. fatty liver
E028. cirrhosis

Gastrointestinal tract - Stomach and duodenal intestine
E029. Acute gastritis
E030. Chronic gastritis
E031. Stomach bleeding
E032. Ulcus ventriculi and duodenal ulcer
E033. Condition after gastric surgery

Gastrointestinal tract - oral cavity and esophagus
E034. Stomatitis
E035. Esophageal carcinoma (esophageal cancer)
E036. Refluosophagitis (heartburn)

Special diseases
E037. Phenylketonuria (PKU)
E038. Rheumatic joint diseases

Metabolism
E039. Obesity (overweight)
E040. Diabetes mellitus
E041. Eating disorders (underweight)

Fat metabolism
E042. Hypercholesterolaemia (increased cholesterol level)
E043. Hepatic Encephalopathy

Heart and circulation
E044. Arteriosclerosis (arterial calcification)
E045. Heart insufficiency
E046. Hypertension
E047. Hyperuricaemia and gout

Changed nutrient requirements
E048. In case of fever
E049. For malignant diseases
E050. After burns
E051. Radiation and chemotherapy

CANCER
E100. Pancreatic cancer
E101. Bladder cancer
E102. Blood cancer (leukemia)
E103. Breast cancer
E104. Colorectal cancer
E105. Gastric cancer
E106. Kidney cancer
E107. Esophageal cancer

TCM
E200. Bladder - moisture heat in the bladder
E201. Bladder - moisture and cold in the bladder
E202. Bladder - emptiness and cold in the bladder
E203. Large intestine - external cold affects the large intestine
E204. Large intestine - moisture heat in the large intestine
E205. Large intestine - heat blocks the intestine II acute
E206. Large intestine - dryness of the colon
E207. Large intestine - Yang deficiency (cold)
E208. Heart - Blood insufficiency
E209. Heart - Blood stagnation
E210. Heart - Fire
E211. Heart - Hot mucus clogs the heart pores

E212. Heart - Cold mucus clogs the heart pores
E213. Heart - Qi deficiency
E214. Heart - Yang deficiency
E215. Heart - Yin deficiency
E216. Liver - Ascending Liver Yang
E217. Liver - Blood deficiency
E218. Liver - Blood stagnation
E219. Liver - Moisture heat in liver and gall bladder
E220. Liver - Fire
E221. Liver - Gall bladder Qi-Empty
E222. Liver - Cold in the liver meridian
E223. Liver - Qi stagnation
E224. Liver - Wind
E225. Liver - Wind with ascending liver Yang
E226. Liver - Wind with blood anemic
E227. Liver - Wind with extreme heat
E228. Lung - Qi deficiency
E229. Lung - Mucus-moisture in the lungs
E230. Lung - Mucus-heat in the lungs
E231. Lung - Mucus-cold in the lungs
E232. Lung - Dryness of the lungs
E233. Lung - Wind-heat attacks the lungs
E234. Lung - Wind-cold affects the lungs
E235. Lung - Yin deficiency
E236. Stomach - Bloodstagnation
E237. Stomach - Fire
E238. Stomach - Cold with liquid
E239. Stomach - Nutrition stagnation
E240. Stomach - Qi deficiency
E241. Stomach - Rebellious Qi
E242. Stomach - Yin Emptiness
E243. Spleen - Heat and moisture attack the spleen
E244. Spleen - Coldness and moisture affects the spleen
E245. Spleen - Qi deficiency
E246. Spleen - Qi deficiency + Declining spleen Qi
E247. Spleen - Qi deficiency + spleen does not control the blood
E248. Spleen - Yang deficiency
E249. Kidney - Heart and kidney no longer communicate
E250. Kidney - Jing deficiency
E251. Kidney - Kidneys cannot receive the Qi
E252. Kidney - Qi is not stable
E253. Kidney - Yang deficiency
E254. Kidney - Yin deficiency

For further information visit di-book.com.